FIVE LITTLE MONKEYS

OVER 50 ACTION AND COUNTING RHYMES

ZITA NEWCOME

WALKER BOOKS
AND SUBSIDIARIES
LONDON • BOSTON • SYDNEY

Contents

Angelina

Yasmin

Charlie

Rosie

Me

Jordan

Yuji

Anna

This collection first published in *Five Little Ducks* (1997)
and *Ten in the Bed* (1999) by Walker Books Ltd
87 Vauxhall Walk, London SE11 5HJ

This edition published 2002

2 4 6 8 10 9 7 5 3 1

This collection and "One Step, Two Step" © 1997, 1999, 2002 Zita Newcome
"Five Big Ice-creams" © Claire Ross-Masson
"The Three Bears" © Hasbro International Inc. Reproduced by permission.
"Here Is the Beehive" by Emily Poulson © J Curwen & Sons Ltd. Reproduced by permission.

Every effort has been made to obtain permission to reproduce copyright material but
there may be cases in which we have failed to trace a copyright holder.
The publisher will be happy to correct any omission in future printings.

This book has been typeset in Century Old Style and Goudy Old Style Educational

Printed in Hong Kong

British Library Cataloguing in Publication Data:
a catalogue record for this book is
available from the British Library

ISBN 0-7445-9615-7

Angelina

Yasmin

Charlie

Rosie

Me

Jordan

Yuji

Anna

This collection first published in *Five Little Ducks* (1997)
and *Ten in the Bed* (1999) by Walker Books Ltd
87 Vauxhall Walk, London SE11 5HJ

This edition published 2002

2 4 6 8 10 9 7 5 3 1

This collection and "One Step, Two Step" © 1997, 1999, 2002 Zita Newcome
"Five Big Ice-creams" © Claire Ross-Masson
"The Three Bears" © Hasbro International Inc. Reproduced by permission.
"Here Is the Beehive" by Emily Poulson © J Curwen & Sons Ltd. Reproduced by permission.

Every effort has been made to obtain permission to reproduce copyright material but
there may be cases in which we have failed to trace a copyright holder.
The publisher will be happy to correct any omission in future printings.

This book has been typeset in Century Old Style and Goudy Old Style Educational

Printed in Hong Kong

British Library Cataloguing in Publication Data:
a catalogue record for this book is
available from the British Library

ISBN 0-7445-9615-7

Number One,
Touch Your Tongue

Number one, touch your tongue.

Number two, touch your shoe.

Number three, touch your knee.

Number four, touch the floor.

Number five, learn to jive.

Number six, pick up sticks.

Number seven, point to heaven.

Number eight, open the gate.

Number nine, touch your spine.

Number ten, let's do it again!

The Wheels on the Bus

The wheels on the bus
go round and round,
Round and round,
round and round,
The wheels on the bus
go round and round,
All day long.

The wipers on the bus go
swish, swish, swish…

The horn on the bus goes
beep! beep! beep!…

The people on the bus go
chat, chat, chat…

The children on the bus
bump up and down…

round and round,

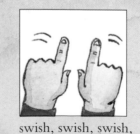

swish, swish, swish,

beep! beep! beep!

The babies on the bus go "WAAH! WAAH! WAAH!"…

The grannies on the bus go knit, knit, knit…

The wheels on the bus go round and round,
All day long.

chat, chat, chat,

bump up and down,

WAAH! WAAH!

knit, knit, knit

Baa, Baa, Black Sheep

Baa, baa, black sheep
Have you any wool?
Yes sir, yes sir, three bags full.
One for the master,
And one for the dame,
And one for the little boy
Who lives down the lane.

Moo, Moo, Brown Cow

Moo, moo, brown cow
Have you any milk?
Yes miss, three jugs smooth as silk.
One for you,
And one for me,
And one for the little cat
Who sits in the tree.

Chook, Chook

Chook, chook; chook-chook-chook,
Good morning, Mrs Hen.
How many chickens have you got?
Madam, I've got ten.
Four of them are yellow,
And four of them are brown,
And two of them are speckled red –
The nicest in the town!

Here's my handle,
here's my spout.

Tip me up and
pour me out!

I'm a tube of
toothpaste...

Lift my lid off
and

squeeze me out!

I'm a Little Teapot

I'm a little teapot, short and stout,
Here's my handle, here's my spout.
When I see the teacups, hear me shout:
Tip me up and pour me out!

I'm a tube of toothpaste on the shelf,
I get so lonely all by myself,
When it comes to night-time, hear me shout:
Lift my lid off and squeeze me out!

Pat-a-cake

Pat-a-cake, pat-a-cake, baker's man,
Bake me a cake as fast as you can.
Pat it and prick it and mark it with B,
And put it in the oven for baby and me.

Pat-a-cake,
pat-a-cake…

Pat it

and prick it and
mark it with B,

And put it in the
oven for baby
and me.

*Tickle as you
say the last line.*

15

Five Cream Buns

Five cream buns in teddy's shop,
Teddy's shop, teddy's shop,
Five cream buns in teddy's shop
Round and fat with a cherry on top.
Along came *(insert your child's name)*
Hungry one day,
She bought a cream bun
And took it away.

Four cream buns in teddy's shop…
Three cream buns in teddy's shop…
Two cream buns in teddy's shop…

One cream bun in teddy's shop,
Teddy's shop, teddy's shop,
One cream bun in teddy's shop
Round and fat with a cherry on top.
Along came *(insert your child's name)*
Hungry one day,
She bought a cream bun
And took it away.

Five Big Ice-creams

Five big ice-creams
With sprinkles on the top.
Five big ice-creams
With sprinkles on the top.
And if teddy takes one
And gobbles it all up –
There'll be how many ice-creams
Standing in the shop?

Four big ice-creams…
Three big ice-creams…
Two big ice-creams…

One big ice-cream
With sprinkles on the top.
One big ice-cream
With sprinkles on the top.
And if teddy takes one
And gobbles it all up –
There'll be no big ice-creams
Standing in the shop.

Head, Shoulders, Knees and Toes

Sing slowly, then fast

Head, shoulders, knees and toes, knees and toes,
Head, shoulders, knees and toes, knees and toes,
And eyes and ears and mouth and nose,
Head, shoulders, knees and toes, knees and toes.

Five Little Monkeys

Five little monkeys jumping on the bed,
One fell off and bumped his head,
Mummy phoned the doctor and the doctor said,
"No more monkeys jumping on the bed!"

Four little monkeys…
Three little monkeys…
Two little monkeys…
One little monkey…

Five little
monkeys…

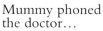

and bumped
his head,

Mummy phoned
the doctor…

"No more monkeys
jumping on
the bed!"

*Repeat actions
showing one fewer
finger each time,
as you count
down.*

Ten Fat Sausages

Ten fat sausages
sizzling in the pan…

One went POP!

and another went
BANG!…

Ten fat sausages sizzling in the pan,
Ten fat sausages sizzling in the pan.
One went POP! and another went BANG!
There were eight fat sausages sizzling in the pan.

Eight fat sausages sizzling in the pan,
Eight fat sausages sizzling in the pan.
One went POP! and another went BANG!
There were six fat sausages sizzling in the pan.

Six fat sausages sizzling in the pan…

Four fat sausages sizzling in the pan…

Two fat sausages sizzling in the pan,
Two fat sausages sizzling in the pan.
One went POP! and another went BANG!
There were no fat sausages sizzling in the pan.

Jumping Beans

One, two, three, four,
Beans came jumping through the door.
Five, six, seven, eight,
Jumping up onto my plate.

Incey Wincey Spider

Incey Wincey Spider
Climbed up the water spout.
Down came the rain
And washed poor Incey out.
Out came the sun,
And dried up all the rain.
So Incey Wincey Spider
Climbed up the spout again.

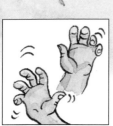

Incey Wincey Spider
Climbed up…

Down came
the rain

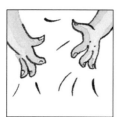

And washed poor
Incey out.

Out came the sun

*Repeat first action as
you sing last line of
the rhyme.*

I Hear Thunder

I hear thunder, I hear thunder,
Hark don't you? Hark don't you?
Pitter patter raindrops, pitter patter raindrops,
I'm wet through, so are you!

I see blue skies, I see blue skies,
Way up high, way up high,
Hurry up the sunshine, hurry up the sunshine,
We'll soon dry, we'll soon dry.

I hear thunder…

Pitter patter
raindrops,

…I see blue skies,
Way up high…

We'll soon dry,
we'll soon dry.

23

Round and Round the Garden

Round and round the garden,
Like a teddy bear,

One step, two step,

Tickle you under there!

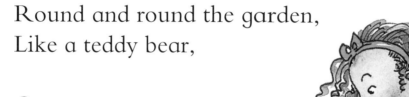

Mouse in a Hole

A mouse lived in a little hole,
Lived softly in a little hole,

When all was quiet, as quiet as can be ...
OUT POPPED HE!

There Was a Little Turtle

There was a little turtle,

He lived in a box.

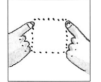
He swam in a puddle,

He climbed on the rocks.

He snapped at a mosquito,
He snapped at a flea.
He snapped at a minnow,
He snapped at me.

He caught the mosquito,
He caught the flea.
He caught the minnow,

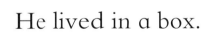
But … he didn't catch me!

Hickory, Dickory, Dock

Hickory, dickory, dock,
The mouse ran up the clock.
The clock struck one,
The mouse ran down,
Hickory, dickory, dock.

Hickory, dickory, dock,
The mouse ran up the clock.
The clock struck two,
The mouse said, "Boo!"
Hickory, dickory, dock.

Hickory, dickory, dock,
The mouse ran up the clock.
The clock struck three,
The mouse said, "Whee!"
Hickory, dickory, dock.

Hickory, dickory, dock,
The mouse ran up the clock.
The clock struck four,
The mouse said, "No more!"
Hickory, dickory, dock.

Johnny Taps with One Hammer

Johnny taps with one hammer,
One hammer, one hammer,
Johnny taps with one hammer,
Then he taps with two.

Johnny taps with two hammers…
Then he taps with three.

Johnny taps with three hammers…
Then he taps with four.

Johnny taps with four hammers…
Then he taps with five.

Johnny taps with five hammers…
Then he stops.

When Goldilocks

The Three Bears

When Goldilocks went to the house of the bears
Oh, what did her blue eyes see?
A bowl that was huge,
A bowl that was small,
A bowl that was tiny, and that was all,
She counted them, one, two, three.

went to the house of the bears

When Goldilocks went to the house of the bears
Oh, what did her blue eyes see?
A chair that was huge,
A chair that was small,
A chair that was tiny, and that was all,
She counted them, one, two, three.

Oh, what did her blue eyes see?

A bowl that was huge…

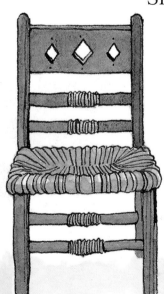

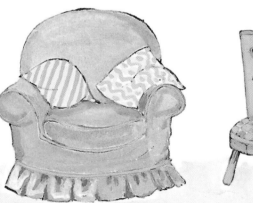

She counted them, one, two, three.

(last verse)

They growled at her, grr, grr, grr!

When Goldilocks went to the house of the bears
Oh, what did her blue eyes see?
A bed that was huge,
A bed that was small,
A bed that was tiny, and that was all,
She counted them, one, two, three.

When Goldilocks ran from the house of the bears
Oh, what did her blue eyes see?
A bear that was huge,
A bear that was small,
A bear that was tiny, and that was all,
They growled at her, grr, grr, grr!

Little Peter Rabbit

Little Peter Rabbit

Little Peter Rabbit had a fly upon his nose.
Little Peter Rabbit had a fly upon his nose.
Little Peter Rabbit had a fly upon his nose.
And he swished it and he swashed it
And the fly flew away.

had a fly upon his nose.

And he swished it and he swashed it

Powder puff and

curly whiskers.

Powder puff and curly whiskers,
Powder puff and curly whiskers,
Powder puff and curly whiskers,
And he swished it and he swashed it
And the fly flew away.

Little Miss Muffet

Little Miss Muffet sat on her tuffet,
Eating her curds and whey.
There came a big spider,
Who sat down beside her,
And frightened Miss Muffet away!

Little Miss Muffet
sat on her tuffet,

Eating her curds
and whey.

There came a
big spider…

And frightened
Miss Muffet away!

Little Miss Tucket sat on a bucket,
Eating some peaches and cream,
There came a grasshopper,
Who tried hard to stop her,
But she said, "Go away or I'll scream!"

"Go away or
I'll scream!"

Two Fat Gentlemen

Two fat gentlemen met in a lane,
Bowed most politely,
Bowed once again.
How do you do,
How do you do,
And how do you do again?

Two thin ladies met in a lane…

Two tall policemen met in a lane…

Two small schoolboys met in a lane…

Two little babies met in a lane…

Two fat gentlemen…

Two thin ladies…

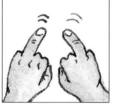

Two tall policemen…

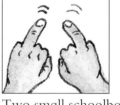

Two small schoolboys…

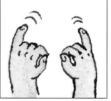

Two little babies…

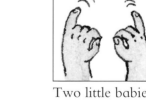

One Man Went to Mow

One man went to mow,
Went to mow a meadow.
One man and his dog,
Went to mow a meadow.

Two men went to mow,
Went to mow a meadow.
Two men, one man and his dog,
Went to mow a meadow.

Three men went to mow…
(you can carry on until you get to ten)

Five fat peas in a peapod pressed,

One grew, two grew

and so did all the rest…

Until one day the pod went POP!

Five Fat Peas

Five fat peas in a peapod pressed,
One grew, two grew and so did all the rest.
They grew and grew and did not stop,
Until one day the pod went POP!

One Potato

One potato, two potato,
three potato, four,
Five potato, six potato,
seven potato, more.

Five Little Leaves

Five little leaves so bright and gay
Were dancing about on a tree one day.
The wind came blowing through the town,
Oooooo … oooooo.
One little leaf came tumbling down.

Four little leaves so bright and gay…
Three little leaves so bright and gay…
Two little leaves so bright and gay…

One little leaf so bright and gay
Was dancing about on a tree one day.
The wind came blowing through the town,
Oooooo … oooooo.
The last little leaf came tumbling down.

Five Little Firemen

Five little firemen standing in a row;
One, two, three, four, five, they go.
Hop on the engine with a shout,
Quicker than a wink the fire is out!

Four little firemen standing in a row;
One, two, three, four, Whoosh! they go.
Hop on the engine with a shout,
Quicker than a wink the fire is out!

Three little firemen standing in a row;
One, two, three, Whoosh! Whoosh! they go…

Two little firemen standing in a row;
One, two, Whoosh! Whoosh! Whoosh! they go…

One little fireman standing in a row;
One, Whoosh! Whoosh! Whoosh!
Whoosh! he goes.
Hops on the engine with a shout,
Quicker than a wink the fire is out!

No little firemen standing in a row;
Whoosh! Whoosh! Whoosh!
Whoosh! Whoosh! they go.

One Step, Two Step

One step, two step, find my teddy bear,
Three step, four step, going up the stair.
Five step, six step, now start to hop,
Seven step, eight step, come to a stop!
Nine step, ten step, going very fast,
Eleven step, twelve step, how long can it last?
Thirteen, fourteen, going very slow,
Fifteen, sixteen, not so far to go.
Seventeen, eighteen, nearly at the chair,
Nineteen, twenty, have a rest with bear.

Teddy Bear, Teddy Bear

Teddy bear, teddy bear, touch your nose,
Teddy bear, teddy bear, touch your toes,
Teddy bear, teddy bear, touch the ground,
Teddy bear, teddy bear, turn around.

Teddy bear, teddy bear, climb the stairs,
Teddy bear, teddy bear, say your prayers,
Teddy bear, teddy bear, turn out the light,
Teddy bear, teddy bear, say goodnight!

Here Is the Sea

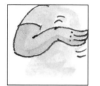

Here is the sea, the wavy sea.

Here is a boat, and here is me.

And all the fishes down below,

Wriggle their tails and away they go.

One, Two, Three, Four, Five

One, two,
Three, four, five,

Once I caught a fish alive.
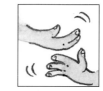

Six, seven,
Eight, nine, ten,

Then I let him go again.

Why did you let him go?
Because he bit my finger so.

Which finger did he bite?
This little finger on the right.

When I Was One

When I was one I ate a bun
The day I went to sea;
I jumped aboard a sailing ship
And the captain said to me:
"We're going this-way, that-way,
Forwards and backwards, over the deep blue sea.
A bottle of rum to fill my tum
And that's the life for me."

When I was two I buckled my shoe…

When I was three I hurt my knee…

When I was four I fell on the floor…

When I was five I learned to dive…

When I was one

I ate a bun…

I jumped aboard
a sailing ship

And the captain
said to me:

"We're going
this-way,

that-way,

Three Jelly Fish

Three jelly fish, three jelly fish,
Three jelly fish, sitting on a rock.
One fell off! … Ooooooo … SPLASH!

Two jelly fish, two jelly fish…
One jelly fish, one jelly fish…

No jelly fish, no jelly fish,
No jelly fish, sitting on a rock.
One jumped up! … Hooray!

One jelly fish, one jelly fish…
Two jelly fish, two jelly fish…

Three jelly fish, three jelly fish,
Three jelly fish, sitting on a rock.
One fell off! … Ooooooo … SPLASH!…

Forwards

and backwards,

over the deep blue sea.

A bottle of rum

to fill my tum

And that's the life for me."

43

The Elephant

The elephant goes like this, like that,
He's terribly big, and he's terribly fat.
He has no fingers, he has no toes,
But goodness gracious, what a nose!

The elephant goes
like this, like that,

He's terribly big,

and he's
terribly fat.

…what a nose!

Boa Constrictor

I'm being eaten by a boa constrictor,
A boa constrictor, a boa constrictor,
I'm being eaten by a boa constrictor,
And I don't like it one little bit!

Oh no! He's up to my toe,
Oh gee! He's up to my knee,
Oh fiddle! He's up to my middle,
Oh heck! He's up to my neck,
Oh dread! He's over my head!
GULP!

Oh no! He's
up to my toe,

Oh gee! He's
up to my knee,

Oh fiddle! He's
up to my middle,

Oh heck! He's
up to my neck,

Oh dread! He's
over my head!

45

Row, Row, Row Your Boat

Row, row, row your boat gently down the stream,
Merrily, merrily, merrily, merrily, life is but a dream.

Rock, rock, rock your boat gently to and fro,
Watch out! Give a shout, into the water you go!

Row, row, row your boat down the jungle stream,
If you see a crocodile, don't forget to scream!

Row, row, row
your boat…

Rock, rock, rock
your boat…

…into the
water you go!

…don't forget
to scream!

Mr Crocodile

Three little monkeys swinging from a tree,
Teasing Mr Crocodile, "You can't catch me!"
Along came Mr Crocodile, quiet as can be … SNAP!

Two little monkeys swinging from a tree,
Teasing Mr Crocodile, "You can't catch me!"
Along came Mr Crocodile, quiet as can be … SNAP!

One little monkey swinging from a tree,
Teasing Mr Crocodile, "You can't catch me!"
Along came Mr Crocodile, quiet as can be,
SNAP! … "MISSED ME!"

Three little monkeys

swinging from a tree,

Teasing Mr Crocodile…

…SNAP!

"MISSED ME!"

Oats and Beans and Barley Grow

Oats and beans and barley grow,
Oats and beans and barley grow,
And not you, nor I, nor anyone know,
How oats and beans and barley grow.

First the farmer sows his seed,
Then he stands and takes his ease.
He stamps his feet and claps his hands
And turns around to view the land.

Oats and beans and barley grow…

Oats and beans
and barley grow,

First the farmer
sows his seed,

Then he stands
and takes his ease.

And turns around
to view the land.

Dingle Dangle Scarecrow

When all the cows were sleeping
And the sun had gone to bed,
Up jumped the scarecrow
And this is what he said:

I'm a dingle dangle scarecrow
With a flippy floppy hat!
I can shake my arms like this,
I can shake my legs like that!

When the cows were in the meadow
And the pigeons in the loft,
Up jumped the scarecrow
And whispered very soft:

I'm a dingle dangle scarecrow…

When all the hens were roosting
And the moon behind a cloud,
Up jumped the scarecrow
And shouted very loud:

I'm a dingle dangle scarecrow…

I'm a dingle dangle
scarecrow

With a flippy
floppy hat!

I can shake my
arms like this,

I can shake my
legs like that!

49

This Little Piggy

This little piggy went to market,

This little piggy stayed at home,

This little piggy had roast beef,

This little piggy had none.

This little piggy went…

Wee, wee, wee,
all the way home!

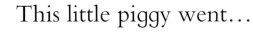

*Run fingers up
arm and tickle!*

Five Little Ducks

Five little ducks went out one day,

Over the hills and far away,

Mother Duck said, "Quack, quack, quack, quack,"

But only four little ducks came back.

Four little ducks went out one day…
Three little ducks went out one day…
Two little ducks went out one day…

One little duck went out one day,
Over the hills and far away,
Mother Duck said, "Quack, quack, quack, quack,"
And all the five little ducks came back.

Here Is the Beehive

Here is the beehive
But where are all the bees?
Hiding away where nobody sees.

Here they come creeping
Out of their hive,
One and two and three, four, five.

Two Little Dickie Birds

Two little dickie birds sitting on a wall,
One named Peter, one named Paul.
Fly away, Peter! Fly away, Paul!
Come back, Peter! Come back, Paul!

Five Little Froggies

Five little froggies sitting on a well,
One looked up and down he fell,
Froggies jumped high,
Froggies jumped low,
Four little froggies dancing to and fro.

Four little froggies sitting on a well…
Three little froggies sitting on a well…
Two little froggies sitting on a well…

One little froggy sitting on a well,
One looked up and down he fell,
Froggy jumped high,
Froggy jumped low,
No little froggies dancing to and fro.

The Animals Went in Two by Two

The animals went in two by two,
Hurrah! Hurrah!
The animals went in two by two,
Hurrah! Hurrah!
The animals went in two by two,
The elephant and the kangaroo.
And they all went into the ark,
For to get out of the rain.

The animals went in three by three,
Hurrah! Hurrah!
The animals went in three by three,
Hurrah! Hurrah!
The animals went in three by three,
The wasp, the ant and the bumble-bee.
And they all went into the ark,
For to get out of the rain.

The animals went in four by four…
The great hippopotamus stuck in the door…

The animals went in five by five…
They felt so happy to be alive…

The animals went in six by six…
They turned out the monkey because of his tricks…

The animals went in seven by seven…
The little pig thought he was going to heaven…

The animals went in eight by eight…
The slithery snake slid under the gate…

The animals went in nine by nine…
The rhino stood on the porcupine…

The animals went in ten by ten…
And Noah said, "Let's start again!"

Walking Through the Jungle

Walking through the jungle,
What do you see?
Can you hear a noise?
What could it be?

Ah well, I think it is a snake, Sss! Sss! Sss!
I think it is a snake, Sss! Sss! Sss!
I think it is a snake, Sss! Sss! Sss!
Looking for his tea.

Walking through the jungle…
Ah well, I think it is a tiger, Roar! Roar! Roar!…

Walking through the
jungle,

What do you see?

Can you hear
a noise?

What could it be?

I think it is a
snake…

Looking for
his tea.

56

Walking through the jungle…
Ah well, I think it is a monkey, Ooo! Ooo! Ooo!…

Walking through the jungle…
Ah well, I think it is an elephant, Stomp! Stomp! Stomp!…

Walking through the jungle…

Ah well, I think it is a crocodile, Snap! Snap! Snap!
I think it is a crocodile, Snap! Snap! Snap!
I think it is a crocodile, Snap! Snap! Snap!
Looking for his tea…

HOPE IT ISN'T ME!

I think it is a tiger…

I think it is a monkey…

I think it is an elephant…

I think it is a crocodile…

Looking for his tea…

HOPE IT ISN'T ME!

Five Bananas

Five bananas on banana tree,
Three for you and two for me.
Five bananas on banana tree
Oh! I love those bananas!

Four bananas on banana tree,
Two for you and two for me.
Four bananas…

Three bananas on banana tree,
Two for you and one for me.
Three bananas…

Two bananas on banana tree,
One for you and one for me.
Two bananas…

One banana on banana tree,
Half for you and half for me.
One banana…

No bananas on banana tree,
None for you and none for me.
No bananas on banana tree
Oh! I love those bananas!

Three Elephants

One elephant went out to play
Upon a spider's web one day.
He thought it such a tremendous stunt
That he called for another little elephant.

Two elephants went out to play
Upon a spider's web one day.
They thought it such a tremendous stunt
That they called for another little elephant.

Three elephants went out to play
Upon a spider's web one day.
The web went CREAK, the web went CRACK
And all of a sudden they all ran back.

Ten in the Bed

There were ten in the bed
And the little one said,
"Roll over! Roll over!"
So they all rolled over
And one fell out,
And he gave a little scream
And he gave a little shout, "Yahoo!"
Please remember to tie a knot in your pyjamas,
Single beds are only made for
One, two, three, four, five, six, seven, eight –

There were nine in the bed…
Please remember to tie a knot in your pyjamas,
Single beds are only made for
One, two, three, four, five, six, seven –

There were eight in the bed…
There were seven in the bed…
There were six in the bed…
There were five in the bed…
There were four in the bed…
There were three in the bed…

There were two in the bed
And the little one said,
"Roll over! Roll over!"
So they both rolled over
And one fell out,
And he gave a little scream
And he gave a little shout, "Yahoo!"
Please remember to tie a knot in your pyjamas,
Single beds are only made for one.
Single beds are only made for one.

Angelina

Yasmin

Charlie

Anna

Yuji

Jordan

Melissa

Rosie

Sam